MIGRATION IN THE SEA

All animals migrate. A migration is any planned journey from one place to another. This book describes some interesting and extraordinary migrations ranging from a few metres to several thousand kilometres.

MIGRATIONS

MIGRATION IN THE SEA

Liz Oram
and
R. Robin Baker
Department of Environmental Biology
University of Manchester

YOUNG LIBRARY

First published in 1991 by
Young Library Ltd
3 The Old Brushworks
56 Pickwick Road
Corsham, Wiltshire SN13 9BX

© Copyright 1991 Young Library Ltd
All rights reserved

ISBN 1 85429 009 6

Printed and bound in Hong Kong

Contents

Introduction 6

1. Animals on the Rocky Shore 9
Sea Anemones, Winkles,
  Blennies, and Gobies 10
Barnacles 12
Limpets 13

2. Moving Home 15
Fighting for a New Home 15
Rock Pool Fish 16

**3. Travelling on the Ocean
   Currents** 17
Barnacles 17
Cod-fish 18

4. Moving with the Seasons 20
Sea Urchins 21
Migrating Down the Shore 22
Crabs and Rock Pool Fish 22
The Californian Sea Lion 22

**5. Long-Distance Seasonal
   Migrations** 25
Lobsters and Prawns 26

Tuna Fish 27
Danger from Fishermen 28
The Walrus 28
Floating Nurseries 28
Whales 29
Humpback Whales 31

6. Leaving the Sea 3
Sea Turtles 3
Eggs Buried in the Sand 33
What happens to the
  Mothers? 35
The Green Turtle 36
The Salmon 37
A Feast for the Grizzly Bear 39
Going Home 40
The Mystery of the Freshwater
  Eel 41
A Mysterious
  Disappearance 43

Glossary 44
Bibliography 45
Picture Sources 45
Index 46

Introduction

Every year thousands of whales set off on journeys that are often as long as 20,000 kilometres. They start in the cold, northern and southern oceans and end in the warmer seas near the Equator.

Whales are not the only sea animals that make journeys. Many

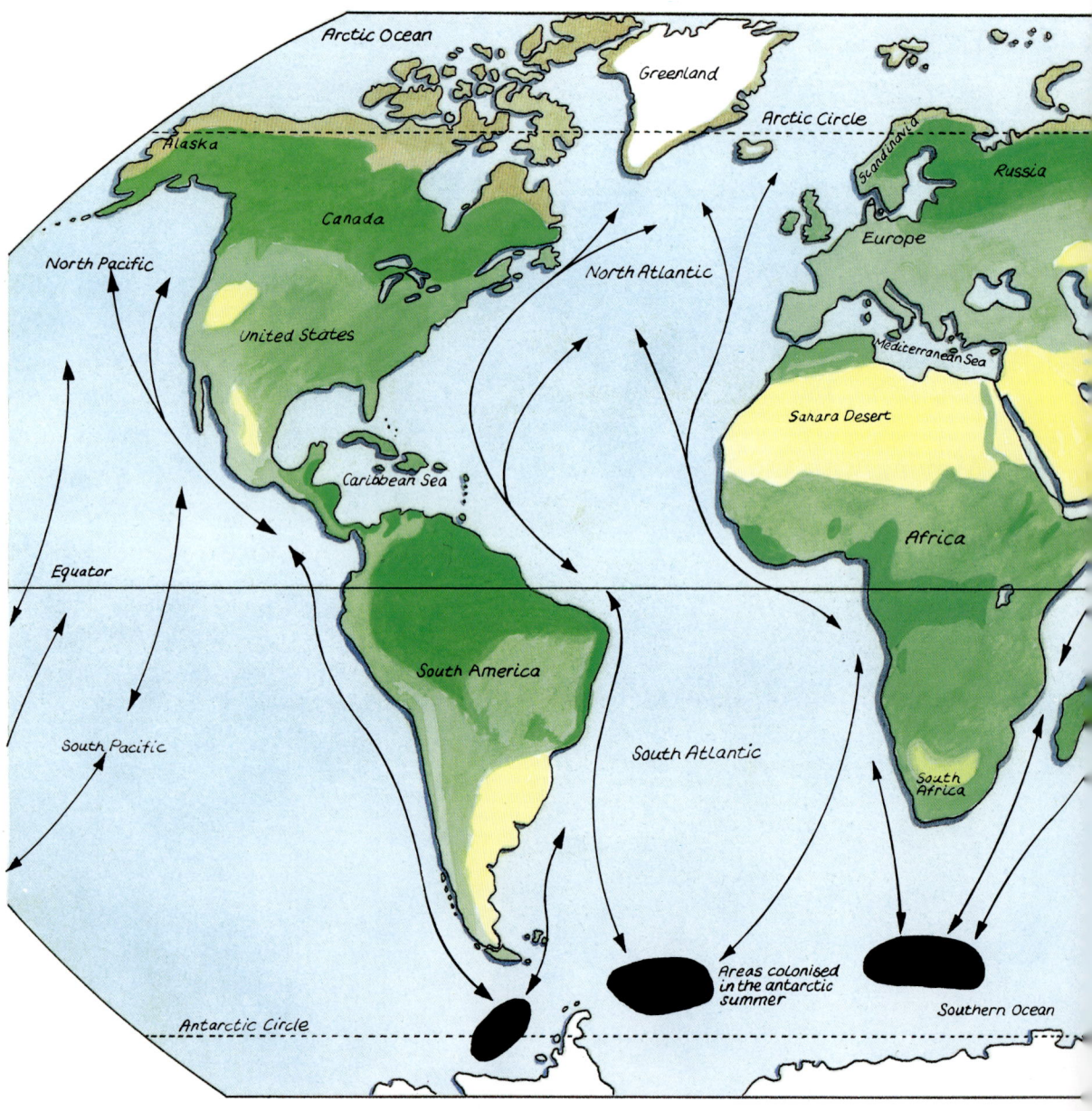

animals, some of them no bigger than a pinhead, regularly make journeys of hundreds of kilometres. In fact, the sea is full of animals making journeys. Some are just below the waves, others are far beneath the surface. Some are on their way to the shore. Others, like the whales, are heading for different waters. Some, like the salmon, are on their way to inland rivers.

Animals that make journeys are called 'migrants'. The journeys they make are called 'migrations'. Sea animals migrate in many different ways. Tuna fish, for example, migrate in large groups called 'shoals'. When shoals of tuna pass through shallow waters, the surface of the sea swells with the movement of these shiny, gliding fish. Other sea animals, like the turtle, migrate thousands of kilometres on their own. Not all sea animals migrate by swimming, though. There is a type of lobster that migrates by walking in a long procession along the sea bed!

It is not easy to watch sea animals migrating. Some migrants, such as whales, have to come up to the surface every so often to breathe. We can at least catch a glimpse of them as they emerge briefly through the waves. We can see other migrants, like the turtle, as they get near to the shore. Only people who have been trained to dive deep down into the oceans are able to see more.

For many of us, this makes migration in the sea even more interesting and wonderful than the migrations of mammals, birds, and insects on land and in the air.

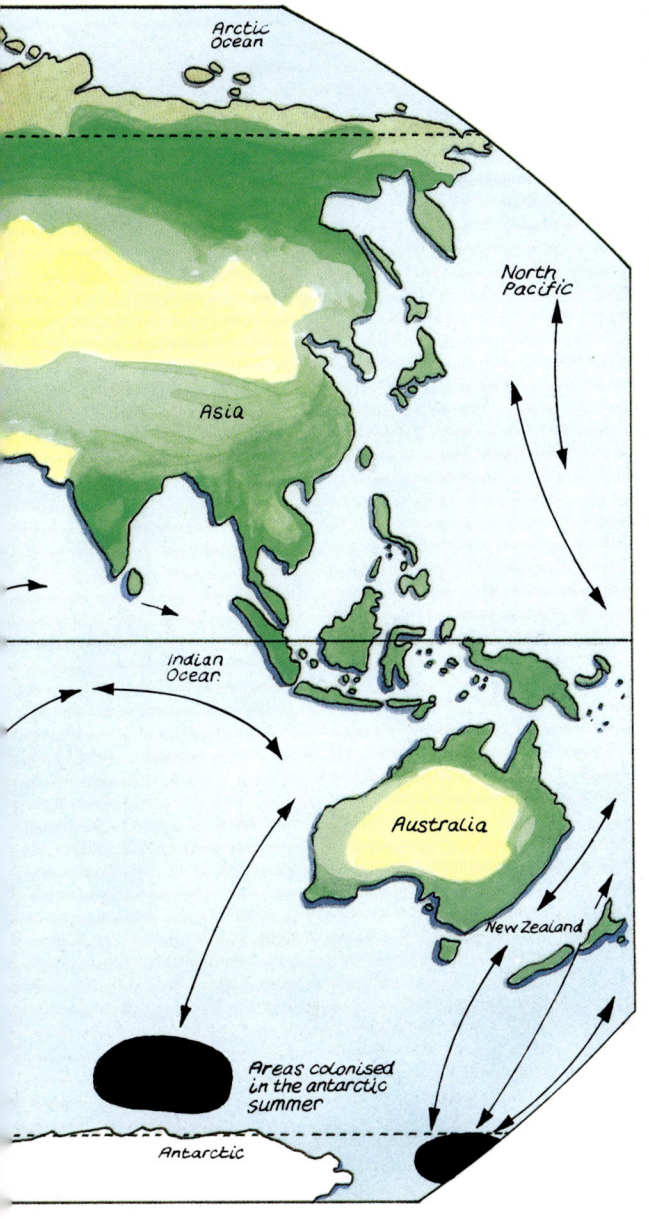

This map shows the migration routes of the Humpback whale. Humpbacks are found in all oceans. They migrate to polar waters in summer to feed, and back to tropical waters in winter.

7

The Blue whale is the largest creature that has ever lived. Only a small part of it shows here, where it has risen to the surface to breathe.

1 Animals on the Rocky Shore

A rocky shore is one of the most exciting places to explore. Perhaps you can remember clambering over rocks and peering into rock pools on a visit to the coast. Did you notice that the rocks were often covered in tiny animals? Some of them look just like shells, others feel slimy to the touch. The rock pools are also teeming with life. Perhaps you saw a tiny fish dart across a pool. As well as fish, in some rock pools there are animals which look just like flowers. These are called 'Sea Anemones'.

In this chapter we are going to look at all these different animals. They all have a fixed home, and most of them make only tiny migrations in order to find food. Some, like the Barnacle, cannot move at all.

Rock pools come in all shapes and

Ebbtide in Monterey Bay, California. Thousands of tiny creatures will now seek a hiding place until the next tide.

sizes. Some are no bigger than puddles. Others can be several metres across. Water collects to form rock pools whenever the rock is shaped like a basin or a saucer. This water has been left behind from the last time the rocks were covered by the tide. When the tide is in, all the rock pools are under water. As the tide goes out the rocks are uncovered, but sea water stays in every hollow to form rock pools.

This rock pool is home to the creatures you see here. They will migrate between tides, but always return.

Most of the creatures in rock pools were not 'left behind' by the tide. The pool is their home and they will still be there after the next tide. During high tides, they migrate.

Sea Anemones, Winkles, Blennies, and Gobies

These are the odd-sounding names of just a few of the animals that live in rock pools. Sea anemones are beautiful, strange animals that look just like flowers. Brightly coloured in reds, greens and blues, they are

These beautiful anemones look like plants, but they are just as much animals as the fish swimming above them.

easy to spot and exciting to find. Sea anemones do not travel very far. Most of the time they are anchored to the rock. They feed on very tiny animals which swim too close, catching them with their long, slender tentacles.

A winkle is a type of snail. Unlike most of the snails which live on land, winkles come in lots of pretty colours. They can be yellow, white, and sometimes even pink.

Some rock pools contain fish. In most parts of the world these fish are called Blennies or Gobies. Some blennies or gobies can grow to a length of twenty centimetres or more. When the tide goes out all of these fish hide in their rock pools. They lie quietly under pieces of seaweed, but if the seaweed is disturbed they dart out across the pool.

When the tide comes in, the rock pool joins with the sea. The winkles crawl out of their pool and roam around on the surrounding rock, looking for food. Winkles have tongues shaped like nail files. They use them to scrape off the tiny plants that grow on the surface of the rock. Winkles can tell when the tide is going to go out again. They always make sure they are back in their

rock pool before the falling tide leaves them stranded on the dry rocks.

The blennies and gobies also come out of their rock pools when the tide is in. They may swim many metres away to find food. Like the winkles, though, they always make sure they are back home before the tide falls.

Barnacles

If you live near a coast you might have noticed the grey-coloured, sharp shells that cluster on many of the rocks. Have you ever tried to pull any of them off? If you have, you will know that they are stuck fast. This is because there is an animal living inside the shell.

This animal is the barnacle. The barnacle lives inside its shell in much the same way as a tortoise does. It produces a sticky substance which glues the shell to the rock.

When the tide is high it covers the rocks. When the tide goes down, water is left in the hollows of the rocks, forming rock pools.

Barnacles are found on rocky shores all over the world. Sometimes the rocks are completely covered in them. They can be packed so tightly that smaller barnacles actually sit on the top of larger ones. Some barnacle shells are so small that they can hardly be seen. Others may be as big as two or three centimetres across.

A barnacle is an animal that stands on its head and kicks food into its mouth with its legs! If you look closely at a barnacle shell you will see a slit at the top. When the tide is out this slit is tightly closed. It stops the barnacle inside from getting too dry. Barnacles die if they become too dry. When the tide comes in the barnacle opens this slit and waves its legs in the water. They are very

Barnacles on a South African beach. They cluster so thickly that there can be thousands of them in a square metre.

hairy and look a bit like a fan. When it does this, it is feeding.

Floating around in the sea are lots of tiny plants and animals. Some are so small that they can only be seen with a microscope. These tiny plants and animals are called 'plankton'. The barnacle's legs are just right for netting plankton. The barnacle sweeps its legs through the water and down towards its mouth. There it sucks off its legs the plankton it has caught. Then it sweeps its legs again through the water to catch some more. When the tide falls the barnacle has to stop feeding. It tucks its legs back into its shell and goes to sleep until the tide comes in again.

Barnacles stick their shells on to rocks very firmly. Once a barnacle is attached to a rock, it never moves. Surprisingly, though, as you will read later, some barnacles travel hundreds of kilometres before attaching themselves to rocks.

Limpets

This animal is a type of snail. It is dark brown in colour, and feels slimy to the touch. Limpets are found on rocky shores all over the world. Sometimes they have barnacles growing on their shells. Unlike barnacles, though, which are stuck to the rock and cannot move, limpets can walk around whenever they want to. Just like land snails they have one big, flat foot. When the tide is in they glide over the rocks on their foot.

However, when the tide is out, the limpet has to hold on to its rock very tightly. Large birds like gulls like to eat limpets. They pull the limpets from the rocks, turn the shells upside down, and eat the animal underneath. The gull has to work very hard, though, to pull the limpet off its rock. Each limpet has a

Over several years, limpets grind homes out of the rock. Each of these shallow pits belongs to one particular limpet.

13

You can see where this limpet fed, by the track it left behind. But now the tide is out and the limpet is back in its home.

special place on the rock where it sleeps when the tide is out. Gradually, over months, the limpet grinds down the surface of the rock to make a small dent. This dent fits the limpet's shell exactly. It is called the limpet's 'depression'. The limpet lives in its depression, making it very difficult for the gull to get a grip.

When the tide is in and the limpet is covered with water, it leaves its home depression and wanders off to find food. Just like the winkle, it has a tongue shaped like a nail file. The limpet uses its tongue to scrape food off the rocks. While it is feeding, the limpet may travel as far as a metre from its home. It is very important that the limpet gets home before the tide falls. As soon as the rocks are exposed, birds start looking for the few unlucky limpets that have not reached home in time.

Limpets can tell when the tide starts to fall. They begin to feel their way back over the rock, just like you would if you were blindfolded. Limpets learn how every part of their rock feels. They also learn how different parts of their rock smell. They guide themselves home by feeling and smelling the rock surface.

2 Moving Home

Sometimes, the rocky shores becomes a difficult place in which to live. In summer, when the sun shines for long periods, the rocks and sand can get very hot. You may have noticed this yourself. People often burn their feet when the sand is very hot. Sometimes the water in rock pools becomes too hot for the fish, or it may even dry up completely. In winter the rocks get very cold and are sometimes covered in ice. In stormy weather waves crash on to the rocks, and some of the animals in the pools may get battered about.

Animals that live on the rocky shore soon realise if they have made their home in a bad place. In this chapter, we shall see what they do when their homes become too uncomfortable.

Barnacles are 'glued' to the rock. They cannot move home. If a barnacle's rock becomes unbearably hot or cold, or if the waves crash too hard, it will eventually die.

Limpets do not like having to leave their homes. It often takes a limpet several years to grind out its home depression. If the animal moves it will have to start grinding out a new one. It will also have to learn how to find its way home to a different place. A homeless limpet is likely to be attacked by birds as it searches for a new home.

However, limpets are crafty animals. They try to make moving home as easy for themselves as possible. Often they will try to steal another limpet's home depression. The homeless limpet moves slowly on to the other limpet's rock. Then, usually when this other limpet is out feeding, it launches an attack. Instead of trying to race back to its depression, the other limpet usually fights.

Fighting for a New Home

A limpet fight is very strange to watch. They fight by butting each other very, very slowly. They look as if they are fighting in slow motion. Each limpet tries to get the edge of its shell under the shell of the other. When this is done, the loser is lifted up high into the air and forced off the rock. Usually, of course, the bigger limpet wins.

When a limpet steals the home of another, the new depression is not a perfect fit. The new limpet has to grind the rock to fit its own shell. However, this is still faster than starting from the very beginning.

The tiny goby lives under rocks in tidepools. A goby's memory of its habitat is so good that it can make its way up and down the beach at low tide by jumping from one pool to another, even though it cannot see the pool it is jumping to.

Rock Pool Fish

In very hot weather many rock pools overheat. The fish which live in them become very uncomfortable, so move to deeper or shadier pools. An overheated blenny or goby moves home in a very spectacular way. It literally jumps from its old rock pool into a new one. Sometimes they jump as far as two or three metres over the bare rock. They hardly ever make mistakes and land between two pools. This is very clever because a fish cannot see the rock pool it is jumping into. So how does it know which direction to jump?

The answer is that the fish makes preparations. When the tide is in, all the rock pools are under water. The fish explores all the dips and basins around its home rock pool. It knows where all the neighbouring rock pools will be when the tide goes out again. Amazingly, it remembers the direction and distance of all these nearby pools. This is how it knows where to jump.

3 Travelling the Ocean Currents

Things that float in the water never stay completely still. They are carried along by the ocean currents. If you sit in a small rowing boat on the sea and do not row, the boat is carried along by the current. Rowing against the current is very hard work. Rowing with the current, however, is much easier. It is almost like having a free ride. Some currents go in more or less straight lines for thousands of kilometres. Others go round in enormous circles thousands of kilometres across. Some currents just go round and round in small bays, while others travel a few kilometres along coasts before becoming very weak.

In this chapter we are to look at a few animals that use the ocean currents to help them migrate.

Barnacles

Some barnacles travel hundreds of kilometres before glueing themselves to rocks. A new-born barnacle is called a barnacle 'larva'. A barnacle larva is very tiny and has no shell, but it can swim. It is born when the tide is in and the parent barnacle is covered with water. This tiny animal swims around in the water and gets carried out to sea by the current. Here, it becomes part of the 'plankton' that we looked at earlier.

The barnacle larva remains as plankton for a few weeks, feeding on

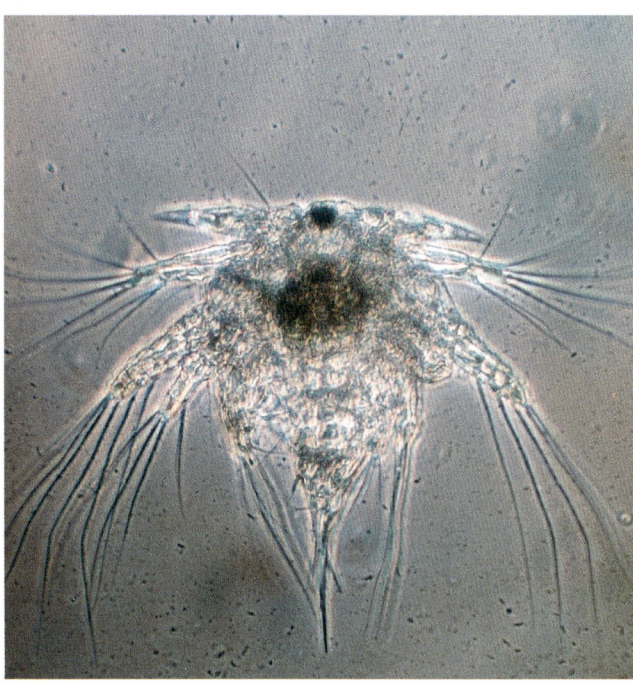

The barnacle larva may migrate hundreds of kilometres in currents. But when ready to become adult it glues itself into place on a rock, and never moves again.

other plankton. If the larva is lucky, the water current will eventually carry it to another rocky shore. This new shore may be hundreds of kilometres from the one where it was

17

born. When it lands on a rock, the larva stands on its head, glues itself to the rock surface and starts to grow a shell. Soon it looks just like a tiny adult barnacle.

The barnacle larva is not the only type of larva that uses water currents to reach new shores. Crabs, lobsters, sea urchins and starfish also produce larvae that float along in the current.

Codfish

Codfish live in the Atlantic Ocean, and are very good to eat. Great numbers of cod are caught in massive nets drawn along through the sea. For most of their life, cod swim among the plankton and are carried along by the currents. When they are young and small they feed on the tiny animals that live in the plankton. Older cod eat other fish, such as herring.

The codfish lays an amazing number of eggs. In one year a single cod can lay as many as 15 million! Only a very few of these eggs reach adulthood, though. The eggs float in the water and are carried along in the plankton by the current. Most of them are eaten by all sorts of sea creatures. After a few weeks the eggs hatch into young cod, and are preyed upon by other fish. When they are about six months old, they drop down to the bottom of the sea for a year or so. Here they feed on tiny crabs and prawns. Eventually, when they are fully grown, they swim up to join the older cod again.

Cod spend most of the rest of their lives swimming along in the ocean currents. They are very clever and

Cod never cease migrating. Young cod change habitat according to size and their ability to avoid predators. Adults move from inshore waters in winter to deeper water in summer. They make long journeys, such as from Newfoundland to Greenland.

18

swim in currents that go in the direction they want to migrate.

Cod are quite big fish. They can grow to a length of 2 metres and weigh more than 90 kilograms when fully grown. Yet they still find it easier to swim with the ocean currents, rather than against them. However, cod are not the biggest animals that use ocean currents to get an easy ride. The tuna fish may grow to a length of four metres and often weighs as much as 450 kilograms. Sea turtles may be nearly two metres long and have a very heavy shell. Even these strong animals use the ocean currents to help them migrate. You can find out more about these two animals later on in the book. Even some of the larger sharks use the currents to help them migrate.

4 Moving with the Seasons

Rocky shores are always changing with the seasons. They become hot in summer, cold in winter, and are battered by the tides in spring and autumn. We have already seen how some animals migrate if their homes become too uncomfortable. These animals are living dangerously, though. They wait *until* it becomes uncomfortable before moving. Sometimes they wait too long and die before they can migrate.

In this chapter, you will read about animals that do not take this risk. They move *before* conditions become uncomfortable. They migrate to cooler places to spend the summer, and to warmer places to spend the winter. They also migrate to avoid being short of food. Some of them, like the sea urchins, crabs, and rock pool fish, are quite small and only move up and down the

People fortunate enough to go diving can see marine creatures in their natural habitat. This plant-like creature is in fact a white-tipped featherstar.

20

shore. Others, like sea lions, are much larger and migrate between the shore and the sea.

Sea urchins move on protruding tubefeet with suckers. On taking a grip, the front feet shorten, pulling the urchin forward.

Sea Urchins

Perhaps you have often been warned of the dangers of swimming in the sea. But has anyone ever warned you about sea urchins? The round-shaped sea urchins are entirely covered in very sharp spines, rather like hedgehog spines. Some sea urchins grow as large as footballs. Others stay quite small, but even the smallest have spines.

The spines are very brittle. If you accidentally step on a sea urchin, the sharp spines stick into your foot and then break off. They are very difficult to remove. It is no good trying to pull them out because they just keep breaking. You just have to wait until the spines drop out by themselves. This can take a very long time.

If you look closely at a sea urchin under water, you will see amongst the spines thousands of long, thin, and fleshy threads. Although they look very fragile, these threads are quite strong. They are the animal's arms and legs. Those underneath the animal have suckers on their ends. They reach forward, stick themselves to the surface of a rock, and pull the sea urchin along. The ones on the animal's back and sides have a mixture of suckers and pinchers on their ends. These keep the animal's spines and back clean by picking off any bits that land on it.

Some sea urchins use their suckers to put seaweed and stones on their back. This makes it more difficult for birds such as sea-gulls to spot them. Sea-gulls like to eat sea urchins. They carry them into the air, then drop them on to the rocks so that they break open. The bird then eats the inside. Sometimes fish with specially protected mouths will also eat the sea urchin.

Migrating Down the Shore

Sea urchins live very low down on the shore. They are left above the water only when the tide goes out a very long way. Sea urchins do not like to be above the water for long in case they are spotted by sea-gulls. Also, they die very easily if they get too hot and dry, or too cold. So most sea urchins migrate down the shore for summer and winter. The further down the shore they go, the less likely they are to be left above the water when the tide goes out.

In spring, many types migrate back up the shore. At this time of year, there are lots of things on the rocks for them to eat. Also, they are not likely to get too hot or cold.

Crabs and Rock Pool Fish

Crabs use their vicious-looking claws for more than just pinching people's toes. They use them to catch and crack open their food. Crabs are particularly fond of snails. They try to make their homes in a place where there are lots of snails for them to eat. As snails move around throughout the year, so do the crabs. They migrate from one home to another at various times of the year, depending on where most snails are to be found.

Some gobies and blennies live in rock pools only during the spring and summer. In autumn and winter the water in rock pools often freezes over. To avoid the frozen rock pools, many blennies and gobies migrate down the shore. Here, just like the sea urchins, they live among rocks that are always under water. In winter it never gets as cold in the sea as it does in rock pools.

The Californian Sea Lion

If California is your home, you may have been lucky enough to see this magnificent animal in the wild. For most of us, though, the only way of catching a glimpse of the Californian

A rock crab from Malindi on the Kenyan coast, about to transfer prey to its mouth. Crabs follow snails, their favourite food.

sea lion is to go to the zoo.

In the wild, Californian sea lions have different homes at various times of year. From May to December they live on small islands along the Californian coast. These small islands are known as 'nursery' homes. From May to July, thousands of females haul themselves up on to the beaches to give birth. Sea lions are very heavy animals. It takes a lot of time and effort for each female to drag herself on to the beach. Each female has just one baby. Soon after giving birth she will mate again so that another baby is produced the following year.

From July to December the islands are just like an enormous nursery. The new-born cubs stay on shore and feed on their mothers' milk. There are thousands of them, all flopping around in the sand and barking loudly at the world. Not all the cubs survive, though. Those that get in the way of fighting males are

23

often crushed to death. A cub can even be crushed to death by its own mother as she rolls around in the sand.

The baby feeds on its mother's milk until about December. Then it starts to go out to sea with its mother and learns how to catch fish. Eventually the mothers stop producing milk, and the young sea lions have to catch all their own fish. Soon after this the mother and cub separate.

In winter the islands are not good homes for sea lions. They need to live in the sea where there are lots of fish for them to eat. So males, females, and young migrate, each by themselves, in search of winter homes in the sea. The males often migrate much further than the females. The females nearly always stay within a few tens of kilometres of their home island. The males may migrate several hundred kilometres to the north.

After spending from January to April swimming in the sea and eating lots of fish, the sea lions are well fed and healthy, with sleek and shiny coats. They are ready to migrate back to their island nursery homes.

The Californian sea lion is the smallest of the five sea lion species. Males migrate north for several hundred kilometres.

5 Long-Distance Seasonal Migrations

In the last chapter we looked at a few animals that have different homes at various times of the year. Some, like the sea urchins and rock pool fish, migrated to avoid bad weather. Others, like the crabs and Californian sea lion, migrated to be in the best place to find food.

None of these animals migrated very long distances. To reach their second homes most of them had to migrate no more than a few tens of metres. Even the big Californian Sea Lion had a winter home that was

The Spiny lobster lacks the large claws of other lobsters, but has protective spines and long spiny antennae.

25

often only 100 km or so from its island breeding home. However, not all animals migrate such short distances from one season's home to another. Some have to migrate hundreds or thousands of kilometres.

Lobsters and Prawns

Prawns and lobsters have very strong front claws. They use these claws for catching and crunching up their food. Lobsters are much larger than prawns. Some grow to a length of 70 cm or more, and are very fierce.

Many types of prawns and lobsters stay in the same home all year round. However, the Oriental prawn migrates as far as 700 km between different summer and winter homes. This prawn lives in the Yellow Sea, which is off the coast of China. The Atlantic prawn lives in the shallow waters off the coast of North America. It often migrates as far as 600 km between different homes. These migrants often make use of the water currents, like the animals in Chapter 3. This makes their long journey a little less tiring. However, there is a type of lobster which migrates by walking along the sea bottom! This is the Spiny lobster. The Spiny lobster lives off the coast of Florida

Spiny lobsters of the Floridan coast migrate about 100 kilometres between summer and winter homes. They form up in single file, then actually walk along the sea bed.

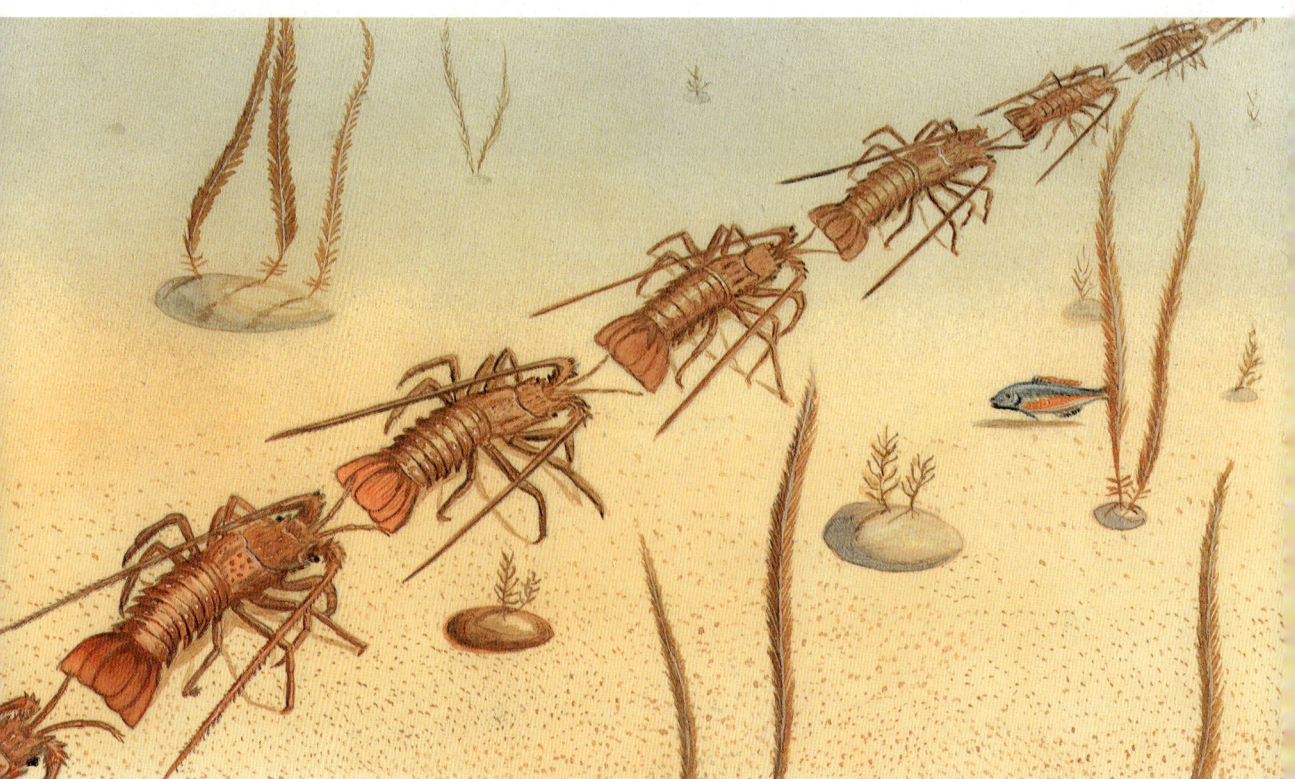

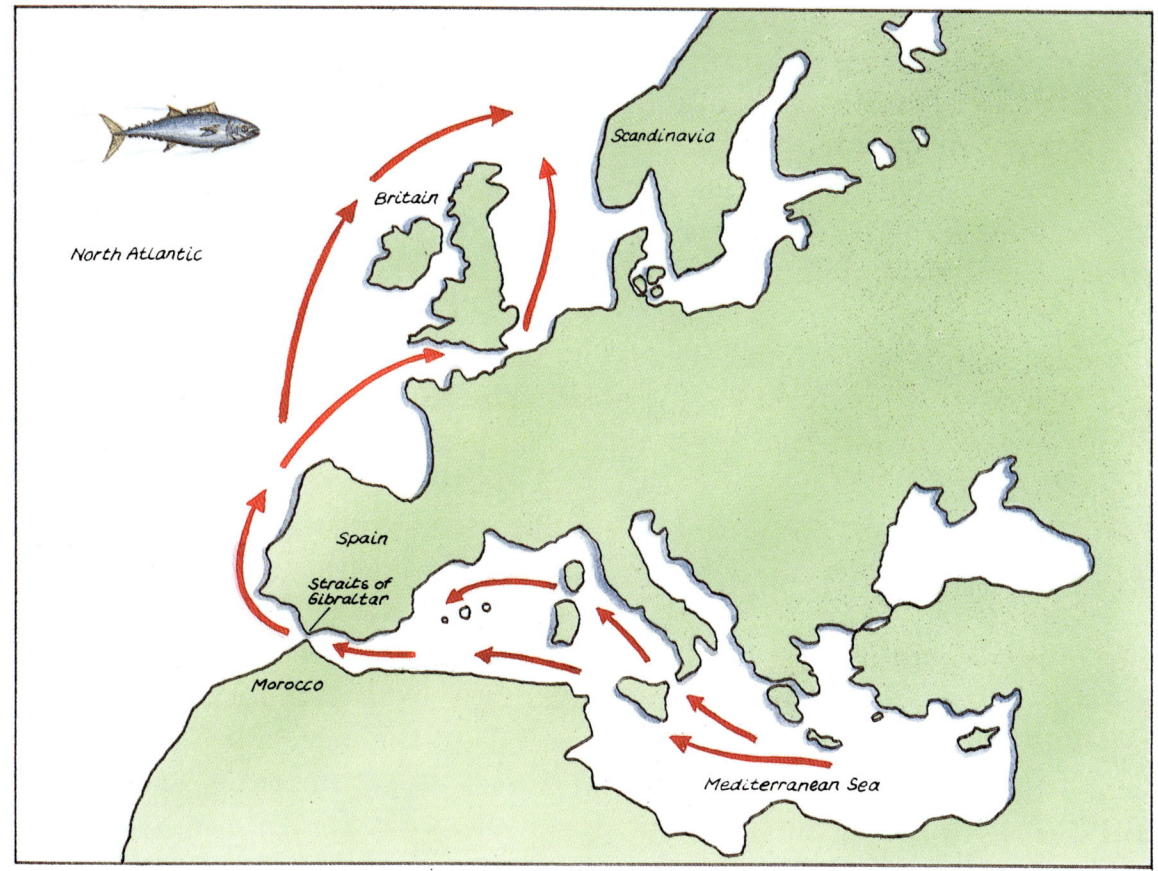

in the United States. Every year it walks about 100 km from its summer home to its winter home.

The migration of the spiny lobster is a remarkable sight. Groups of lobsters get together to form long lines on the sea bottom. There may be as many as 100 lobsters in one line. Each lobster touches the one in front. This strange procession then marches off down the coast to warmer waters.

Tuna Fish

This fish is also called the 'Bluefin Tuna', or just the 'Tunny'. The Tuna fish is a magnificent animal. It has a beautiful dark blue back,

Every year the Mediterranean tuna streams through the Straits of Gibraltar. During its 4000–5000 km journey it will travel up to 250 kilometres per day.

silvery sides, and large gold spots on its fins. The adult is usually about 2.5 metres long, but some can grow to 4 metres — about twice the height of a man.

The Tuna feeds on other, smaller fish like Sardines, Anchovies, Mackerel, and Herring. It will also eat larger fish like cod. Tuna are found all across the Atlantic Ocean, from the Gulf of Mexico to the Mediterranean Sea. They are also found in the Black Sea, and in parts of the Pacific Ocean. In the

Mediterranean, the tunny first lay eggs in the sea water when they are three years old. Most of them then migrate out of the Mediterranean. They pass through the narrow gap between Spain and Africa in large shoals. Some shoals contain as many as 10,000 fish. They are heading for their autumn homes around Britain and Scandinavia. Sadly, though, many of these magnificent fish never make it.

Danger from Fishermen

For a migrating tuna fish the greatest danger comes from people. Mediterranean fishermen put out large nets to catch the migrating fish as they pass through the Straits of Gibraltar. The fishermen are nearly always successful. Huge numbers are caught, to end up in tins on the supermarket shelf.

Those tuna that escape the fishermen's nets head north for their autumn homes. They travel very fast. Some migrate as far as 5000 km in just one month, using the ocean currents to help them on their way. They spend the autumn feeding on fish in ocean homes around Britain or Norway. Then, from November onwards, the tuna start to migrate back to the south. This time they travel at a much slower rate. They will pass through the Straits of Gibraltar in spring, and once more the fishermen's nets will be waiting for them.

The Walrus

Most of you will be familiar with this magnificently ugly animal. It looks like a gigantic seal, except that it has a pair of fine tusks, just like the elephant. The walrus lives in the Arctic Circle, near to the North Pole.

The North Pole is in the middle of a large sea called the Arctic Ocean. It is so cold at the North Pole that this ocean is covered by a very thick layer of ice that never melts or breaks. Nothing lives there. In winter, the Arctic ice cap spreads all the way from the North Pole to the coasts of Canada, Greenland, and Russia. In summer, the ice cap shrinks away from these coasts. It leaves a mixture of cold sea water and floating blocks of ice. These floating blocks of ice are called ice 'floes'. Walruses live around the edge of the Arctic ice cap, and use the ice floes as travelling homes.

Floating Nurseries

Walruses usually feed in the morning. They dive off their ice floe into the freezing water. They can dive down to a depth of 100 metres. Like all types of seal, walruses can hold their breath under water for many minutes. They use their tusks to help them uncover shellfish and other food on the sea bottom. They also use their tusks for fighting.

Young walruses are born on

Walruses can migrate lazily by hitching a ride on ice floes. The floes can drift thousands of kilometres southwards from the frozen Arctic seas.

floating ice floes. Female walruses give birth every two years in May or June. The young cub feeds on its mother's milk for a whole year. Even when it is old enough to feed itself, it may stay and travel with its mother for a further two years or more. The young cub will be six years old before it is able to mate.

The ice floes float on the water. They are blown along by the wind and carried along by water currents. Some ice floes are very large, and whole groups of walruses can sit on them. As the ice floe is carried along, the walruses are carried along on it. How far the walruses migrate each year depends on how far the current takes their ice floe. Ice floes can often drift thousands of kilometres.

Sometimes ice floes melt. Sometimes they get stuck amongst ice or on land. Sometimes the ice floats into water that is too deep for the walruses to reach the bottom and feed. If any of these things happen, the walruses swim away and find another ice floe to travel on.

Whales

Whales look like gigantic fish, but they are not fish — they are mammals. They give birth to live young in the water, and feed them on milk from their bodies. Mammals are unable to breathe under water. They have to hold their breath all the time they are under water, just like you and me. Some whales can hold their breath for up to half an hour! When they come up to the surface to breathe, whales blow great jets of spray and water into the air from their noses. The whale's nose is just a hole on the top of its head.

There are two different groups of whales. One group has big teeth, and so are called toothed whales. They feed on animals such as fish, squid, seals, or even other whales. Examples of this type of whale are the Killer whale and the Sperm whale. Killer and sperm whales roam the oceans looking for food. They travel in small herds. Some

KILLER WHALE

HUMPBACK WHALE

BLUE WHALE

To show how big whales are, the child and the elephant are drawn in the same scale.

30

herds migrate thousands of kilometres each year.

Dolphins and porpoises also belong to this group of mammals. They are really just another, smaller type of toothed whale. Dolphins and porpoises also roam the seas in small herds looking for food. However, they do not migrate as far as the killer and sperm whales.

The other type of whale is the baleen whale. Baleen whales do not have teeth. They are the biggest of all animals but, feed on very tiny food called krill, and other plankton. When they feed, baleen whales take in big gulps of water. They have special mouths which sieve the plankton out of the water. After this, the plankton is rolled into a big ball which the whale swallows.

It is amazing that whales can grow to be so big from feeding on such tiny food. A type of baleen whale called the Blue whale is the biggest animal that has ever lived on our planet. A fully grown blue whale is about 25 metres long. This is even bigger than the biggest dinosaur that ever lived!

Humpback Whales

The Humpback whale is a baleen whale. However, it does not grow as large as the blue whale. When fully grown, this whale is about 13 metres long. The humpback whale is found in oceans all round the world, from the Arctic Ocean all the way down to the Antarctic. Look at the map on pages 6 and 7. Each humpback whale has two homes, one for summer and one for winter.

The humpback makes its summer home in the cold waters near to the polar ice. The plankton in these icy waters is very thick. The whales spend the whole summer feeding, and put on a lot of fat. As winter approaches, the ice gradually spreads over the sea. The whales can

SPERM WHALE

no longer come to the surface to breathe, so they begin the long migration to their winter home. In small groups, they swim slowly towards the Equator. There is not much plankton in the seas around the Equator. This means that the whales hardly feed at all during this part of their migration.

In the warm tropical waters near the Equator the whales give birth. Young whales are called calves. After giving birth, the whales mate again to produce the calves that will be born in a year's time. The calves feed on their mother's milk and grow very rapidly. In spring, the mother and calf begin the long journey back to the polar feeding grounds and their summer home. The males begin their return journey about two weeks later.

The Humpback is one of those whales that feed on plankton, which is plentiful in polar seas. But the whales must return to tropical waters to give birth.

Humpback whales make strange and eerie sounds under water. These sounds are known as the 'song' of the humpback whale. Perhaps the whales are talking to each other as they travel. The sounds travel a lot further under water than they would on land. Some scientists believe humpbacks can talk to each other even when they are hundreds of kilometres apart.

6 Leaving the Sea

In the last chapter, we looked at a few animals that spend all their lives on or in the sea. In this chapter we are going to look at a few animals that migrate out of the sea to spend time in other homes. Do you remember the Californian sea lion? This creature spends part of the year in the sea and the rest of the time on land. In this chapter you will read about another strange animal that has one home on land and another in the sea. This is the sea turtle.

We are also going to look at two types of fish that migrate out of the sea and into the fresh water of rivers and streams. Each year, salmon and eels migrate thousands of kilometres between their two homes.

Sea Turtles

Sea turtles are just like huge tortoises. Their shells can measure as much as a metre across, and they sometimes weigh as much as 225 kilograms. On land sea turtles have to drag themselves along by their flippers, but in the water they are quite graceful swimmers. As well as being good swimmers, sea turtles are also able to dive. They can stay under water for long periods, but eventually they have to come up to the surface in order to breathe.

Sea turtles make their homes in the warm waters of tropical seas. Most of the time they stay in the sea and feed on the seaweed which grows along the coasts. They are very long-lived. Some sea turtles live to be over a hundred years old.

Eggs Buried in the Sand

Male sea turtles spend all their lives in the sea. Females are different. Every two or three years, each female has to migrate to a sandy beach in order to lay her eggs. The females stay near the beach for about two months. Then, about every twelve days, in the middle of the night, a very strange spectacle takes place. Hordes of female turtles drag themselves up on to the beach and start to dig holes in the sand with their flippers. When the holes are big enough, each female lays about 100 soft, leathery eggs. The eggs are then covered with sand. Sometimes, so many females try to lay their eggs on the same beach that later females dig up eggs laid earlier. These eggs get cold and eventually die, or they are eaten by birds.

Those eggs which manage to stay buried hatch into tiny sea turtles about two months later. By now the mothers are far away, having swum back out to sea soon after laying their eggs. Each tiny turtle is lucky if it survives the first few days of its life. First, they have to dig their way up through the sand and on to the beach. Once in the daylight they have to run for their lives! Circling above the beach are many birds just waiting for the young turtles to emerge, so that they can eat them.

The amazing thing is that the newly hatched turtles seem to know exactly which direction the sea is in. They scuttle off in the right direction without a moment's hesitation. Even if the sea is obscured by a sand dune the turtles still know which way to go. Sadly, though, many never make it. Some are carried off and eaten by the birds. Others are suffocated as they dig out of the sand. Even the lucky few that do make it to the sea are not completely out of danger.

In the shallow waters near the coast large fish, such as sharks, lie in wait for the baby turtles. Sharks are particularly fond of baby turtles. The plucky little turtles swim out to sea as fast as they can. The further from the shore they can get, the safer they will be. However, what happens to those that manage to escape the sharks' jaws is a mystery.

A Green turtle. Males spend their entire lives in the sea, but females must visit land in order to lay their eggs.

A baby turtle's migration begins at birth, tunneling up through sand, and then a desperate race down the beach to the sea.

Once in the deeper waters, the baby turtles disappear for about one-and-a-half years. Scientists and divers have taken out boats and spent many days searching for them. None have ever been found. Perhaps they hide in the large mats of floating seaweed that are found in all tropical seas. Or perhaps they are just so tiny that trying to find them is as hopeless as looking for a needle in a haystack!

What happens to the Mothers?

After laying their eggs, the mother turtles swim back out to sea. Some of them now have numbers painted on their shells. They have been put there by scientists so that they can recognize the turtles if they see them again. They hope to find out where the mothers go to after they leave the nesting beaches.

Most female turtles seem to swim along with the ocean currents. They use the currents to migrate to their coastal feeding homes. Sometimes the currents take the turtles no further than a few tens of kilometres along the coast from their nesting beaches. At other times the currents take them over a thousand kilometres across entire oceans. For example, the leatherback turtle crosses the North Atlantic. It travels in the Gulf Stream from the Gulf of Mexico, and turns up mainly on the coasts of Britain and Norway.

The Green Turtle

One type of sea turtle is the Green turtle. There is a group of green turtles which lay their eggs on an island in the middle of the Atlantic Ocean. This island is called Ascension Island. These same green turtles have their homes on the coast of Brazil. Every two or three years the females migrate the 2000 kilometres to Ascension Island to lay their eggs.

Ascension Island is only eight

After laying her eggs the turtle returns to the sea. Here a Leatherback paddles away through the Great Barrier Reef.

kilometres across, and lies right in the middle of the huge Atlantic Ocean. The turtles often have to swim against the current in order to reach it. Swimming against the current is very tiring, even for an animal as large as the turtle. Scientists have no idea how the turtles manage to find such a small island in such a huge ocean.

Another thing the scientists do not know for certain is what happens to the babies. Green turtle youngsters do turn up on the coast of Brazil. However, the green turtle nests all over the tropics. We can't be sure that the Ascension Island babies return there.

The Salmon

Salmon are beautiful fish. They are found throughout the northern halves of the Pacific and Atlantic oceans. When they are fully grown, Atlantic salmon are a lovely silvery colour. Several different types of salmon live in the Pacific ocean. When fully grown, some of these types become a bright pink or red. A full-grown salmon is about 70 cm long.

All salmon spend much of their lives in the sea. They migrate with the currents and can sometimes be over 1,000 km from the nearest land. They feed on other, smaller fish, but they themselves are the favourite food of seals and sea lions.

When salmon are fully grown they migrate to the coast. Some may have travelled 4,000 km or so in a big circle with the ocean currents. The Atlantic salmon migrates to the coasts of Europe in the east, and Greenland and North America in the west. Pacific salmon make their way to the coasts of Canada and North

Salmon live in the northern Atlantic and Pacific oceans. When fully grown they migrate to the coasts coloured in red.

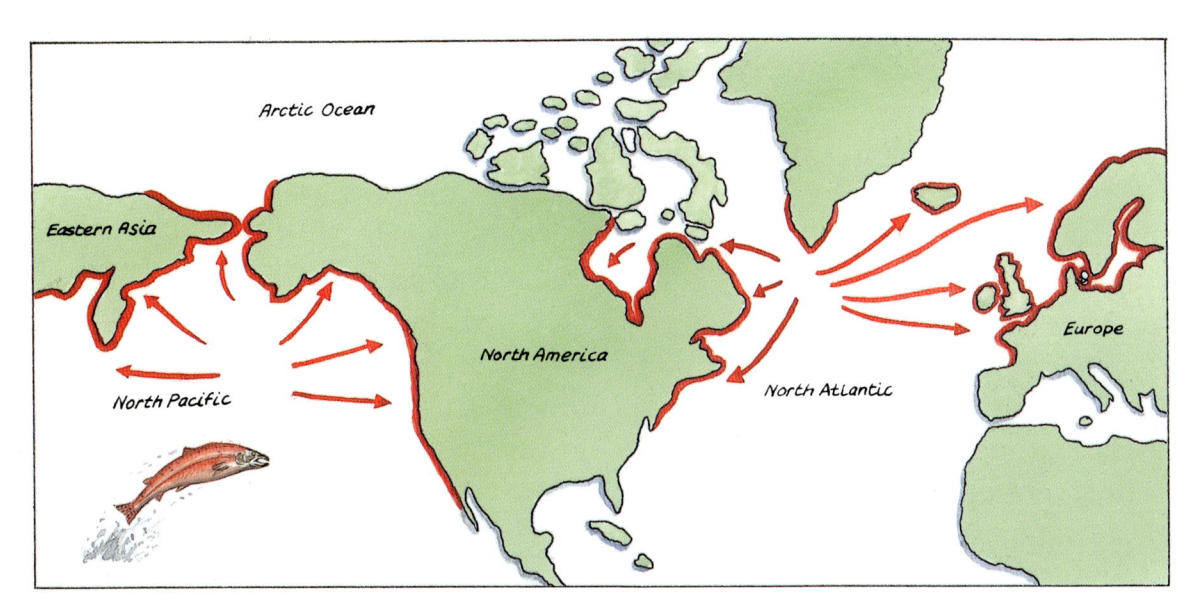

America in the east, and Siberia and Japan in the west.

At the coast the migrants find a river. Lots of salmon crowd together where this river joins the sea. When they are all ready, the fish begin to migrate up the river. They do not stop to feed, and can travel 15 km each day.

Some salmon swim up very long rivers. In Russia, they often make their way up rivers as long as 1,000 kilometres. They are looking for a special place, a good place to lay their eggs. When salmon lay their eggs it is called 'spawning'. Usually, the best places to spawn are a long way upstream, in shallow, clear waters.

The migrating salmon are

Salmon choose a river and surge up it, sometimes for up to 1000 kilometres. If they find a waterfall they leap over it.

unstoppable. As well as swimming through still, quiet lakes, these fish battle their way up fast-flowing streams, struggle against floods, and — most spectacular of all — jump up waterfalls. The only way a salmon can get past a waterfall is by jumping over it. But how does a fish manage to jump into the air?

When they reach the bottom of a waterfall, the salmon back away a few metres. Then they race back towards the base of the waterfall. They start to swim up towards the surface as they get nearer. At the last minute they whip their tails very

In shallow waters the swarming salmon are easy prey for bears, which will often come together to trap them.

fast. This shoots them out of the water and up into the air.

Salmon can leap over waterfalls which are as high as 3.5 metres. This is as high as a man with a young child standing on his shoulders. Often it takes the fish several attempts to jump waterfalls as high as this. When they eventually land on top of the waterfall, the salmon swim quickly away before the current carries them back over the edge.

A Feast for the Grizzly Bear

Waterfalls are not the only hazards faced by migrating salmon. In North America, Black and Grizzly Bears catch the salmon in their enormous paws as they swim past. Sometimes lots of bears gather together and wade in the shallow waters. Most dangerous of all, however, are fishermen. It is a special achievement for an angler to catch a salmon. This makes him try very hard to make one bite his hook.

Eventually, the fish arrive at good places to spawn. In some long rivers it takes the salmon a whole year to swim from the sea to the spawning site. With her tail the female digs a hole in the gravel at the bottom of the stream. This is where she lays her eggs. The eggs are fertilized by the nearest male. The female then covers the fertilized eggs with gravel.

By the time the salmon have spawned, they are exhausted. Most are so exhausted that they die without ever trying to return to the sea. Some, however, have some strength left and begin the long journey back to salty waters. A year or so later they will be battling their way back upstream to the very same spawning grounds. Once in Scotland a 13-year-old salmon was caught. This old fish had migrated backwards and forwards between the sea and the river no less than five times!

Going Home

The salmon eggs take about three months to hatch into tiny fish. In cold places like Scandinavia and northern Canada, the young salmon may stay in their river home for as long as eight years. In warmer places, though, like the United States and Britain, they usually stay for about one year. They feed on the worms and insects that live in the river, and slowly get bigger.

When the young salmon are about 10 centimetres long, they start to migrate downstream towards the sea. Strangely enough, they are

Tiny salmon, still bearing their yolk sacs, swim amongst unhatched eggs in a stream. One day they will return to the sea.

carried along by the current tail first! No one quite knows why this is so. The salmon migrate very slowly. Often they travel no more than about 2 kilometres a day. However, eventually they reach the sea. By now the salmon are a beautiful, shining silver colour.

Salmon are very clever fish. When the time comes to spawn, each fish manages to find its way back to the very same stream in which it was born. How do the salmon know which is their river, when they are in the sea? When they have migrated up the river, how do they recognize the stream in which they were born? The answer is that the salmon use their noses! These fish have an excellent sense of smell. Each river and stream has its own particular

A fish which can travel over land. Although the Atlantic eel lives most of its life in fresh water, it is born in the sea.

scent. Salmon remember the smell of the rivers and streams in which they are born. When they migrate back to these rivers, the salmon really do follow their noses, all the way home.

The Mystery of the Freshwater Eel

An eel is a long fish that looks a bit like a snake. Some eels live always in the sea, but we are going to look at the Freshwater eel. This eel normally lives in lakes and rivers. Sometimes it lives in marshes and

41

swamps. If the ground is very wet, it even wriggles through the grass and undergrowth, just like a snake. The freshwater eel lives in the countries around the North Atlantic Ocean: North America, Britain, Scandinavia, France, Belgium, Holland, and Germany and also around the Mediterranean.

Although the Atlantic eel lives

These elvers have already travelled thousands of kilometres from the Sargasso Sea. Now they swim up an English river.

most of its life in fresh water, it is born in the sea. But nobody knows where. Nobody has ever found an egg of the Atlantic eel. Newly-hatched eels are very flat in shape. They look just like leaves as they float along in the plankton. These tiny flat eels are found in a part of the Atlantic known as the Sargasso Sea. Some people believe that this is where the eels are born, but no one has found an egg to prove it.

Young eels are called elvers. The tiny, flat, leaf-like elvers are gradually carried across the Atlantic Ocean by the currents. It takes them a whole year to migrate from the Sargasso Sea to the coasts of North America. It takes them nearly four years, though, to reach the Mediterranean. By the time they arrive at the coast they look a bit more like eels. However, they are almost transparent and are still no more than a few centimetres long.

The elvers wriggle their way up rivers and streams. They migrate very slowly, feeding as they go. They are too small to jump over waterfalls like salmon. Instead, they have to crawl up the wet stones at the side of the waterfall. As they crawl they look like thin, white worms. Eventually they find a suitable home in a lake or river, and by now they have grown into eels.

A Mysterious Disappearance

Eels often stay in their freshwater homes for as long as fifteen years. During this time they grow slowly until they reach a length of about 50 centimetres. Then they become very restless and start to swim downstream towards the sea. As

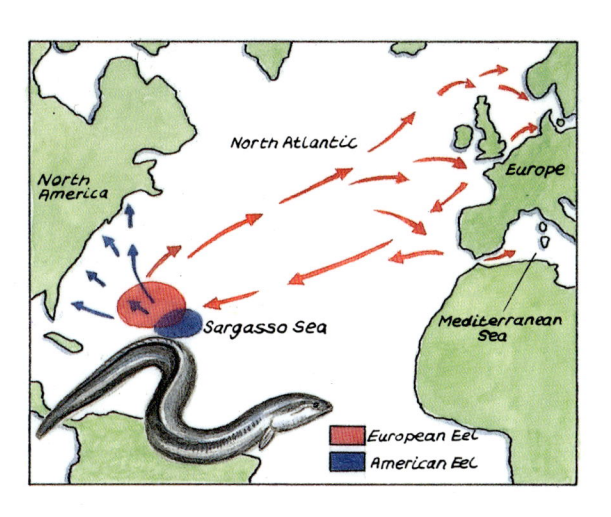

Eels are born in the Sargasso Sea. Some turn left for America, identical ones turn right for Europe. Yet by the time they arrive they can be identified as different species.

they go, they change colour from a yellowish grey to a really fine silvery colour. Also, their eyes begin to grow larger and larger. When the eels reach the sea they swim quickly away from land. Then they start to swim deeper, using their enlarged eyes to help them see in the dark waters. They swim deeper, and deeper, and deeper... then they disappear.

Scientists have tried to follow the eels at sea to find out where they go. They have hired big boats with all sorts of expensive equipment to try and track them. So far, the eels have always escaped being followed. Nobody knows what happens to the eels or where they go. Perhaps they go back to the Sargasso Sea, lay their eggs, and die. Or perhaps they live for many more years deep at the bottom of the Atlantic Ocean. Nobody knows.

Glossary

Antarctic The whole area of the globe lying to the south of $66\frac{1}{2}$ degrees south latitude.
current A steady flow of wind or water that moves faster than the surrounding wind or water.
egg The form of life in which many creatures, including fish and reptiles, first appear from their mothers' bodies. They are usually produced in vast numbers, and drift in the water until they hatch.
Equator The (imaginary) line around the centre of the globe separating the northern and southern hemispheres. Most the earth's hottest regions are at sea-level on the equator. There is no winter or summer.
fertilize To make eggs capable of growing and developing by joining them with male sperm.
freshwater Water which is not salty, as it is in the sea.
Gulf Stream A warm current which flows from the Gulf of Mexico northeastwards to north-west Europe.
habitat The type of place where a particular plant or animal naturally lives.
herd A number of wandering mammals living together as a group.
home The habitat of those sea creatures which are not wanderers.
ice cap The thick mass of ice that permanently covers the polar regions.
mammal All creatures whose young feed on milk from the mother's body.
mating A female animal joining with a male animal to produce eggs or live young.
migrant/migrate/migration The habit of moving from one habitat to another (usually in search of food) is called *migration*. An animal that *migrates* is a *migrant*.
north The direction a compass needle points. Most maps are drawn so that the northernmost part is at the top.
North Pole The northernmost point of the Earth. It is surrounded by ocean covered with permanent ice.
plankton Tiny creatures, some too small to be seen, which drift on the surface of the sea, and upon which other creatures feed.
polar Polar regions are the regions around the North and South Poles where it is always icy and very cold.
Sargasso Sea An area of the North Atlantic (see map on page 43) covered in floating brown vegetation.
shoal A large number of fish of the same kind swimming together.
south The direction opposite to north.
spawn The mass of eggs deposited in the water by fish and some other creatures.
tide The twice daily rise and fall of the sea on a shore. It is caused by the gravitational pull of the sun and moon.
tropics An area around the centre of the earth reaching $23\frac{1}{2}$ degrees either side of the Equator. Within this band, about 5,500 km wide, the climate is very hot.

Bibliography

MIGRATION
Adult books which older children would enjoy

Baker, R.R., *The Mystery of Migration* (Macdonald)

Ricard, Matthieu, *The Mystery of Animal Migration* (Constable)

NATURAL HISTORY
Children's books containing some information on migration

Bramwell, Martin, *Oceans* (Franklin Watts)
Henry, T.E., *Seashore* (Granada)
Jennings, Terry, *Sea and Seashore* (O.U.P.)
Padgett, Sheila, *Coastlines* (Wayland)
Parsons, James, *Oceans* (Macdonald Educational)
Schutz, Siegfried, *Fish Calendar* (A & C Black)

Picture Sources

ARDEA: Francois Gohier cover and 8, 24, 32, 38; Stefan Meyers 39; P. Morris 18–19; 25, 34; Ron Taylor 21; Ron and Valerie Taylor 36; Alan Weaving 23.

Bruce Coleman: Jane Burton 41, 42; Adrian Davies 16 upper; Jeff Foott 9; David Hughes 35; M. Timothy O'Keefe 20; Freider Sauer 17; Bernd Thies 29; Gunter Ziesler 13 upper, 14.

Simon Girling Associates/Richard Hull: cover inset, 6–7, 10, 12, 13 lower, 16 lower, 26, 27, 30–31, 37, 43.

ZEFA: S. Frink 11; Orion Press 40

Index

A
anemones, *see* Sea anemones
Antarctic Ocean 31, 44
Arctic Ocean 28, 31
Ascension Island 36
Atlantic eel, *see* Freshwater eel
Atlantic Ocean, 18, 27, 36–7, 42–3
Atlantic prawn 26

B
Baleen whale 31
barnacle 9, 12–13, 15, 17–18
Belgium 42
birth
    Californian sea lion 23
    Humpback whale 32
    salmon 40
    sea turtle 33
Black Sea 27
blenny 11–12, 16, 22
Bluefin tuna, *see* tuna
Blue whale 31
Brazil 36
Britain 28, 36, 40, 42

C
California 23
Californian sea lion 22–4
Canada 28, 37, 40
China 26
cod 18
crab 18, 22
crustaceans
    barnacle 12–13
    crab 18–22
    krill 31
    lobster 18, 26–7
    Oriental prawn 26
    prawn 18, 26
    Spiny lobster 26–7

currents 17–19, 37, 43, 44
    see also Gulf Stream

D
dolphin 31

E
echinoderms
    Sea urchin 21–2
    starfish 18
eel, *see* Freshwater eel
elver 43
Europe 37

F
fish
    blenny 11–12
    cod 18
    elver 43
    Freshwater eel 41–3
    goby 11–12, 16, 22
    salmon 2, 37–40
    shark 19
    tuna 19, 27–8
fixed homes 9–14, 15–16
Florida 26–7
France 42
Freshwater eel 41–3

G
Germany 42
Gibraltar, Straits of 28
goby 11–12, 16, 22
Greenland 28, 37
Green turtle 36–7
Gulf of Mexico 27, 36
Gulf Stream 36, 44

H
Holland 42
Humpback whale 31–2

J
Japan 38

K
Killer whale 30
krill 31

L
larvae
    barnacle 17
    crab 18
    lobster 18
    Sea urchin 18
    starfish 18
limpet 13–14, 15
lobster 26

M
mammals
    baleen whales 31–2
    Blue whale 31
    Californian sea lion 22–4
    dolphin 31
    Humpback whale 31–2
    Killer whale 30
    porpoise 31
    Sperm whale 30
    toothed whales 30–31
    walrus 28–9
mating 44
    Californian sea lion 23
    Humpback whale 32
Mediterranean Sea 27–8, 42–3
migration
    alone
        turtle 6
    definition, 2, 6, 44
    drifting
        salmon 40–41
        walrus 28–9

in shoals
   cod 18–19
   Freshwater eel 41–3
   tuna 6, 28
jumping
   goby 16
out of the sea
   Freshwater eel 43
   salmon 38–40
   Sea turtle 33
running
   Sea turtle 34
walking
   Sea urchin 21–2
   Spiny lobster 6, 27
with the tide 10, 11–12, 13, 14
molluscs
   limpet 13–14, 15
   winkle 10–12
mysterious disappearances
   Freshwater eel 43
   Green turtle 37
   Sea turtle 35

N
North America 26, 37–8, 39, 42–3
North Pole 28, 44
Norway 28, 36
nursery homes 23, 28–9

O
Oceans and seas
   Antarctic 31, 44
   Arctic 28, 31
   Atlantic 18, 27, 36–7, 37, 42–3
   Gulf of Mexico 27, 36
   Mediterranean 27–8, 42–3
   Pacific 27, 37
   Sargasso 43, 44
   Yellow 26
Oriental prawn 26

P
Pacific Ocean 27, 37
periwinkle, *see* winkle
plankton 13, 17, 18, 31, 44
polyps
   Sea anemone 9, 10–12
porpoise 31
prawn 18, 26
predators
   crab 22
   Grizzly bear 39
   gull 13, 22
   humans 28, 39
   sea lions 37
   seals 37
   shark 34

R
reptiles
   Green turtle 36–7
   sea turtle 19, 33–5
rock pools 9–14, 15–16
Russia 28, 38

S
salmon 2, 37–40
Sargasso Sea 43, 44
Scandinavia 28, 40, 42
Sea anemone 9, 10–12
sea lion, *see* Californian sea lion
seas, *see* oceans and seas
Sea turtle 19, 33–5
Sea urchin 21–2
shark 19
shore life 9–14, 15–16, 17–19, 20–22
Siberia 38
Spain 28
Sperm whale 30
Spiny lobster 26–7
starfish 18

T
tide 10, 44
tuna 19, 27–8
tunny, *see* tuna
turtle, *see* Sea turtle

U
United States 26, 40, *see also* North America

W
walrus 28–9
whale 6, 29–32
   baleen 31
   Blue 31
   Humpback 31–2
   toothed 30
   dolphin 31
   Killer whale 30
   porpoise 31
   Sperm whale 30
winkle 10–12

Y
Yellow Sea